One, Two, Three, BENE!
A Wish for a Kinder World

One, Two, Three, BENE!

A Wish for a Kinder World

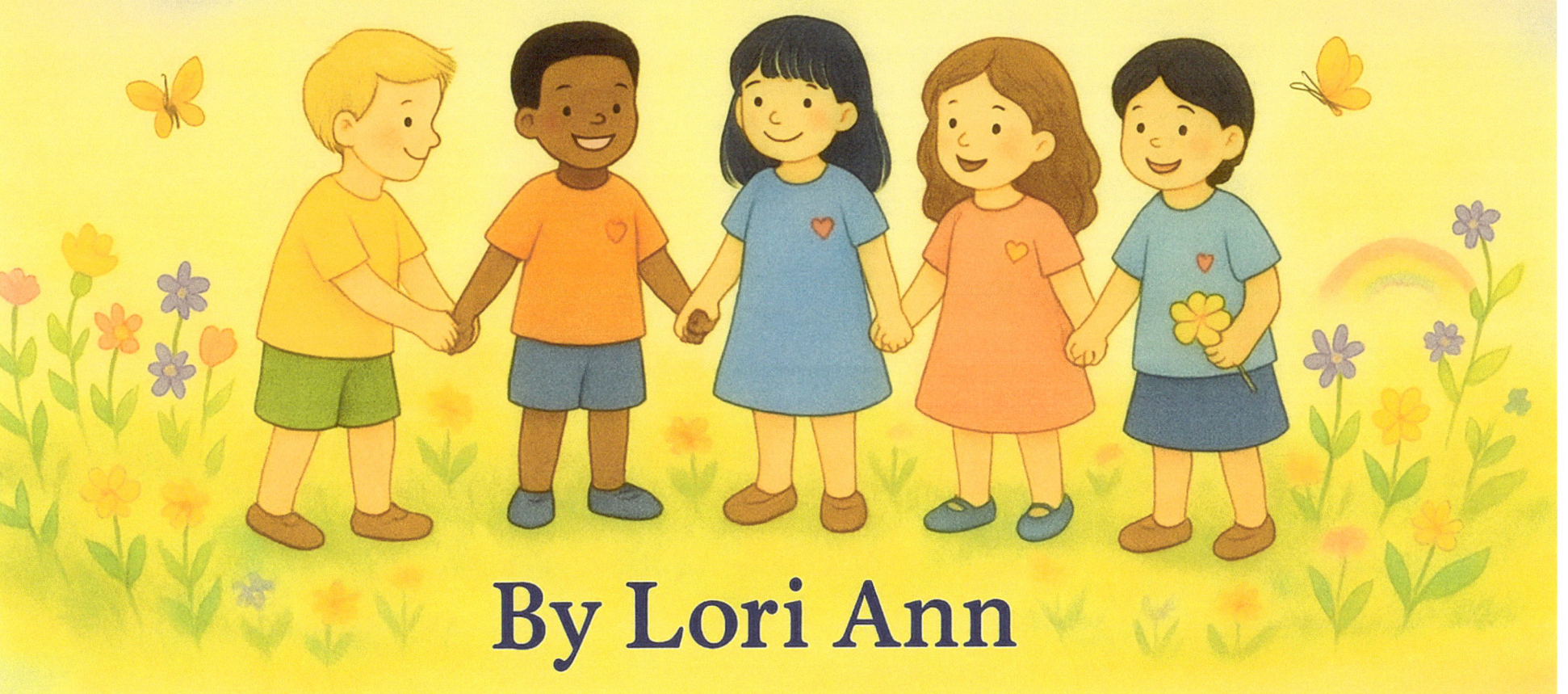

By Lori Ann

One, Two, Three, BENE!
A Wish for a Kinder World
Copyright © 2025
Lori Ann

Comments:
4hoping@gmail.com

ISBN:
979-8-218-82258-3

Published by
still learning, inc.

Dedication

This book was named by a few of my Grands –
Thank You, Reid, Ariella, and Emmy for your wise
counsel on finding just the right title for a book that
will be read by many!

And – To Every One of my Grands – You are my
light and joy. Your smiles are filled with hope and
kindness – and the world needs more of this.

I am so grateful to be your MomMom.

Dear Reader,

Every act of kindness, no matter how small, has the power to brighten someone's day, lift a heavy heart, and bring us closer together.

Bene is one small part of the word Benevolence, it means to "wish another well."

Benevolence means showing care, sharing love, and believing that together we can build a world full of hope, harmony, and humanity.

Reflection Question:

Can you remember a time when someone's kindness made you feel special? What did they do?

Invitation to Practice:

This week, try doing one kind thing each day—maybe draw a picture for someone, help a neighbor, or offer a smile to a friend who feels sad. Together, you can help the sun shine even brighter—for everyone.

Words That Guide Our Hearts

These words help us grow into the kind, caring people we're meant to be. Let them light the way as we build a better world together.

 ## Humanity

Humanity means caring for everyone, treating others with respect.

 ## Hope

Hope is the light in our hearts that helps us believe.

 ## Community

A community is a group of people who help, support, and care for each other.

 ## Harmony

Harmony means living and working peacefully together.

Once upon a time,

where kindness lit the way,
And gentle words were spoken
every single day.

Our minds were full of wonder,
questions we would share,
Dreaming of a brighter world,
built with love and care.

But one day, a dark cloud formed,
blocking out the sun,
Our laughter disappeared,
our joy began to run.

The darkness lingered heavy,
hearts too low to lift;
We forgot the greatest treasure—
our humanity, our gift.

Fear grew in the silence,
like shadows in the night.
We turned away from each other,
instead of holding tight.

Smiles began to vanish,
kindness slipped from view—
The world felt dim and lonely,
as worry only grew.

But humanity's the key,
the light that helps us stand,
To build a world of harmony
across this precious land.

Then came a small voice,
gentle, warm, and true.

Whispering: "Embrace
your humanity —
let the light shine
through."

It will take all our hearts,
working side by side,
To mend what has been broken,
to turn the rising tide.

"Where do we begin?"
another voice asked near.
A raindrop fell in answer—
one shining, tender tear.

The people all looked inward;
the first step now was clear:

They must gather up their
courage and release their fear.

So they met within the square
to chase the cloud away,
And shared small acts of kindness
to brighten up the day.

"One, two, three- BENE!"
they shouted, strong and true.

And to their great surprise,
the sun came shining through!

The warmth upon their faces
brought smiles wide and bright;
They hugged and called out
"BENE!"—their hearts
were full of light.

And in that joyful moment,
the town began to see,
The power of their humanity
to live in harmony.

Together they committed
to build a life that's true –
A Benevolent Community,
with love in all they do.

A future full of promise,
aglow with hope and grace,
A path to guide forever—
every heart, in every place.

A Poem, Blessing my First Grandchild – Reid Jonathan
And one that I have changed, as appropriate, to welcome every one of
my wonderful grandchildren that have followed….

I walked into a room
and there he was
pink wrinkled folds
tiny fingers and toes
perfectly shaped head
adorned with a blue cap
eyes mouth and chin
that I was seeing for the first time
and yet I remembered from long ago
There is no prep course for this moment
no manual that describes the watershed
emotion of meeting one's grandchild
for the very first time
As I picked him up
I felt the threads of past present and future
weaving their magic
to protect this tiny being
How is it that this small human
holds all of life's hopes within him
There are experiences that seem to define
the sum of all our joys and sorrows
achievements and challenges
but none as perfect as having
My son introduce me to His
This is an occasion
where for just a second or two or three

life stands still
to honor the miracle before us
in his first breaths of life
all time is held and recorded
in the perfection of expression
from what I will never fully know
but witness here
Holding my grandson
Feeling the love that glows
From a newborn's face
Is surely heaven on earth
How grateful I am
To share in this miracle
Wrapping him in my arms
I hold all the generations past
And pray that all the days of his life
be blessed with the love that
surrounds him in these few moments
where time has paused to welcome
Reid Jonathan to the world,

By Lori Ann from her book, moving through life: doors and thresholds of past present and future, Prose Press, 2017.
Lori Ann has recently published an adult companion to One, Two, Three, Bene!
Rooted In Humanity – Reclaiming Benevolence in Support of a Community's Coming of Age,
still learning, 2025.
And…There is a Curriculum of Essential Community Conversations and a companion Journal – Rooted In Humanity available
by contacting Lori at 4hoping@gmail.com., both are perfect for Community Organizations, Faith-Based and
Educational Groups.

About the Author: Lori Ann is an experiential educator, retreat and workshop facilitator and leadership coach. She has a deep love for children, teens, and emerging adults and in her forty-year career has had the honor of being in the indoor and outdoor classroom with all age groups from pre-school thru college. Lori's greatest teachers have been her four grown children, their spouses, and her many grandchildren.

She is very excited about this book – it is her first for Children…(of all ages). Lori admires children's books for their timeless and valuable lessons about navigating life – especially in times of challenge. Lori is the founder of a small human centered nonprofit organization, Create Safe Space, whose focus is to Build Benevolent Communities Worthy of Our Shared Humanity. To learn more about the Benevolent Community Initiative, its programs, conversation circles, and retreats contact Lori at director@createsafespace.org or look on the website for more information: www.createsafespace.org.

All proceeds from the sale of this book
go to the
The Benevolent Community Initiative